YOU CHOOSE

Life in the AZTEC EMPIRE

AN INTERACTIVE ANCIENT HISTORY ADVENTURE

BY CLAUDIA OVIEDO

Consultant:
Stephanie M. Strauss, Ph.D.
Ancient Mesoamerican
Art and Writing

CAPSTONE PRESS
a capstone imprint

Published by Capstone Press, an imprint of Capstone
1710 Roe Crest Drive, North Mankato, Minnesota 56003
capstonepub.com

Copyright © 2026 by Capstone. All rights reserved. No part of this publication may be reproduced in whole or in part, or stored in a retrieval system, or transmitted in any form or by any means, electronic, mechanical, photocopying, recording, or otherwise, without written permission of the publisher.

Library of Congress Cataloging-in-Publication Data
is available on the Library of Congress website.

ISBN: 9798875216282 (hardcover)
ISBN: 9798875216251 (paperback)
ISBN: 9798875216268 (ebook PDF)

Summary: The Aztec Empire thrived in central Mexico for nearly 200 years. Its culture was known for its well-designed cities and impressive temples, as well as its skill at conquering neighbors and forming alliances to expand its power. But what was it like to live there during the height of this empire? Explore life as a little priest. Try your hand as a traveling merchant. Work as a tax collector in a conquered town. YOU CHOOSE who to be, where to go, and what to do. Will you succeed? Will you fail? Will you even survive? It's up to you!

Editorial Credits
Editor: Alison Deering; Designer: Bobbie Nuytten;
Media Researcher: Svetlana Zhurkin; Production Specialist: Katy LaVigne

Image Credits
Alamy: Sailingstone Travel, cover (middle); Bridgeman Images: 71, © Bodleian Libraries, University of Oxford, 79, © NPL–DeA Picture Library/G. Dagli Orti, 39, Mexicolore/Sean Sprague, 11, Photo © North Wind Pictures, 102, Photo © NPL–DeA Picture Library, 19; Getty Images: Grafissimo, 4, jejim, cover (bottom left), 8, 14, 42, 72, 100, MattGush, 89, Nastasic, 48, PeterHermesFurian, 6–7, Photos, 60, rawfile redux, 105, shakzu, 92, Simon McGill, 53; The Metropolitan Museum of Art: Museum Purchase, 1900, 109; Newscom: imageBROKER/Ian Murray, 30; Shutterstock: Fabio Imhoff, 23, Jose Luis Rocha Pereira (stone doorway), cover, 1, Oksana Belikova, 108, Peter Hermes Furian, 27, WitR, 36; SuperStock: DeAgostini, 25, Iberfoto Archivo, 40

Any additional websites and resources referenced in this book are not maintained, authorized, or sponsored by Capstone. All product and company names are trademarks™ or registered® trademarks of their respective holders.

Printed and bound in China. 6276

TABLE OF CONTENTS

ABOUT YOUR ADVENTURE................ 5
GET TO KNOW THE AZTEC EMPIRE 6

Chapter 1
AN EAGLE LANDS ON A CACTUS 9

Chapter 2
THE SPIRIT OF A PEOPLE.............. 15

Chapter 3
ALL THE LANDS..................... 43

Chapter 4
GROWING DISCONTENT 73

Chapter 5
THE LEGACY OF A FALLEN EMPIRE..... 101

Timeline of the Aztec Empire 106
More About the Aztec Empire 107
The Aztec Empire Today 108
Glossary 110
Read More 111
Internet Sites 111
About the Author 112
Books in This Series 112

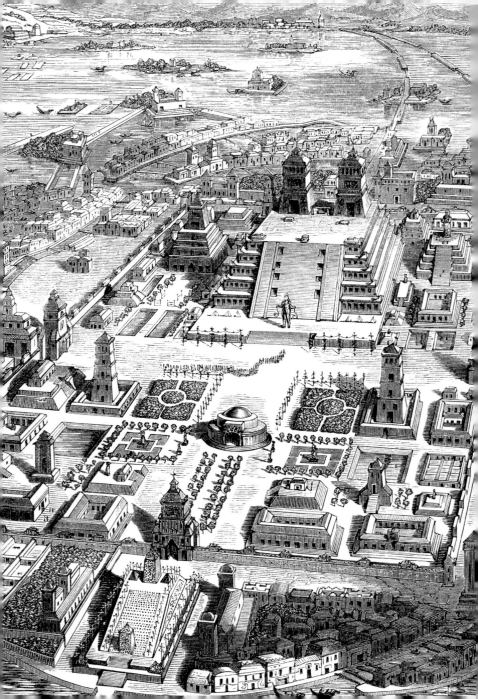

ABOUT YOUR ADVENTURE

YOU are living in the Aztec Empire hundreds of years ago. As a member of this vast ancient civilization, there are many paths to explore. You could experience life as a priest in the late 1300s. Or you could be a traveling merchant in the mid-1400s. You could also be tasked with collecting tributes from your neighbors in the early 1500s.

Whatever you decide, YOU CHOOSE the paths that will fulfill your destiny or seal your fate. How will you make your mark as a member of this remarkable civilization?

Turn the page to begin your adventure.

Get to Know
THE AZTEC EMPIRE

Aztlan (ahs-TLAHN) is the original homeland of the Aztecs. The city is believed to be located somewhere in the southwestern United States.

Aztec (AZ-teck) refers to people who came from Aztlan.

The Aztecs who settled in the the Valley of Mexico began referring to themselves as Mexica (meh-HEE-kah), which means "people of Mexico."

Nahuatl (NAH-wah-tl) was the language spoken in the Aztec Empire.

Tlatelolco
Tlaxcala
Tenochtitlan
Cholula

The tlatoani (tlah-toh-AH-nee) was the ruler or leader of the empire.

A tlamatini (tlah-mah-TEE-nee) was a priest.

The Huey Teocalli (WEH tay-oh-KAH-lee) was the great temple at the center of Tenochtitlan, the empire's capital city.

PACIFIC OCEAN

The Aztec Empire was vast and included many important cities:

  Tenochtitlan (teh-nohch-TEET-lahn)—the capital city of the Aztec Empire
  Tlatelolco (tla-teh-LOHL-koh)—the sister city of Tenochtitlan
  Cholula (cho-LOO-lah)—an independent city and ally to Tenochtitlan
  Cempoala (sem-POH-ah-lah)—a city conquered by the Aztecs
  Tlaxcala (tlahks-KAH-lah)—an independent city and rival to Tenochtitlan

GULF OF MEXICO

○ Cempoala

The Aztecs believed in many gods. The gods were thought to control every aspect of life. Some of the main gods include:

  Huitzilopochtli (wee-tsee-loh-POHCH-tlee)—god of war and fire
  Tlaloc (TLAH-lok)—god of rain
  Mictlantecuhtli (meek-tlan-teh-KOOT-lee)—god of death

Chapter 1

AN EAGLE LANDS ON A CACTUS

Long before the Spanish arrived in the Americas, the Aztecs began their long journey from what is now the southwestern United States. In the two hundred years that followed their departure, they were pushed out of many places. Finally, they stumbled onto an island in the middle of a lake. It was in a place now known as the Valley of Mexico.

By today's calendar, the year was 1325 CE. The only place left to settle was marshy. Still, it had plenty of fish and fruit to eat. The land belonged to the Culhua. They were descendants of the Toltec people who had ruled the area for hundreds of years. The Culhua agreed to let the Aztecs stay.

One day, the Aztecs saw an eagle on top of a cactus. They took it as a sign. They believed one of their gods, *Huitzilopochtli*, wanted them to build a city there. Today, many people believe the eagle was holding a snake. Some people believe that it was a falcon rather than an eagle.

In order to build their city, the Aztecs turned on the Culhua. A war followed. The Aztecs won. They built the city of Tenochtitlan and finally set down roots. This is how they became the Mexica, or people of Mexico.

Once built, Tenochtitlan seemed to rise out of the water. Chinampas, or floating gardens, increased the land for farming. They also provided a base for building homes and other things. Canals crisscrossed the city and served as sources of water. They also served as passageways for merchant canoes. Raised roads connected Tenochtitlan to the rest of the valley. This helped with trade and communication.

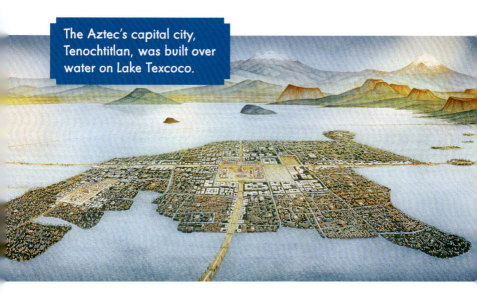

The Aztec's capital city, Tenochtitlan, was built over water on Lake Texcoco.

At the heart of the city lay a walled-off area. This was reserved for temples and the homes of nobility. They showed off their riches in fancy houses with gardens and pools. The tlatoani—or ruler—was Tenochtitlan's highest nobility.

The Huey Teocalli, or great house of god, was a temple that stood at the center of everything. It was dedicated to Huitzilopochtli, god of war and fire, and Tlaloc, god of rain. Two massive staircases led to their temples at the top of the pyramid.

The Aztecs believed in making sacrifices to thank and honor the gods, who they believed had sacrificed themselves for man's existence. They sometimes offered gifts, such as flowers, pottery, and art. Human and animal sacrifices also took place at the Huey Teocalli.

Neighborhoods surrounded the temples. Narrow, winding streets led to busy markets. These were filled with merchants. They sold goods from all corners of the Valley of Mexico and beyond, including turquoise from what is now the American Southwest and jade from the jungles of what is now Guatemala.

Over time, some of the Aztecs moved to an island north of Tenochtitlan. They built their own city—Tlatelolco. This marked the rise of the Aztecs as an empire and a great power.

Between the early 1300s and the early 1500s, the Aztecs went on to fight many wars. They conquered many nearby territories. Instead of always killing or sacrificing those they defeated, they required them to pay tributes, similar to taxes. This supported the empire's growth.

What was life like for people living in the Aztec Empire during this period? What would you do if you were a priest known as a tlamatini? What new places would you see as a traveling merchant, or pochteca? What would it be like to serve as a tax collector, or calpixque, in a conquered town? The time has come to make a choice and find out!

> To be a tlamatini in the late 1300s, turn to page 15.
>
> To be a pochteca in the mid-1400s, turn to page 43.
>
> To be a calpixque in the early 1500s, turn to page 73.

Chapter 2
THE SPIRIT OF A PEOPLE

It's the late 1300s in the city of Tenochtitlan, and flickering torch light illuminates your parents' faces. You sit upon a woven mat in the small chamber. Your mother's hand reaches out and gently touches your shoulder.

"Listen, xilotl . . ." she begins.

You smile at the nickname. You like it when she calls you her small, tender ear of maize.

". . . you have been chosen to follow a path of great honor," your father finishes.

Excitement tightens your stomach. Studying to become a tlamatini—a priest—is a great honor. It is the biggest thing that has happened in your twelve years of life.

Turn the page.

Coming from a family of stone laborers, you never thought you'd be chosen. The role is typically reserved for those from noble families. But your background doesn't matter now. Your teachers have seen something in you.

Your mother's voice interrupts. "It will be hard, but we believe in you."

You nod. The reality of leaving your family is still sinking in. Once you finish your studies, you will go straight into a life of service.

"I will miss you, but I will also try to make you proud," you reply.

The next morning, you wake up before dawn. The sounds of vendors setting up their stalls fill the streets. You make your way past them with your family at your side.

When you arrive at the temple, you hug your parents goodbye. Your sister, Yaretzi, looks ready to cry. You understand her grief—your time as children together is finished.

Your education under a tlamacazqui—an experienced priest—begins. In the days that follow, you learn about the gods and their roles. You grow to understand how the calendar systems work. They are used for the ceremonies and farming cycles.

You learn the sacred dances, rituals, and ceremonies. You chant ancient prayers and make offerings. You spend hours studying omens and signs. There is something special about the flight of birds, the patterns of clouds, and the movements of stars. You learn to interpret messages in dreams and in visions.

At times, learning is physically hard. To purify yourself, you fast for days. You are hungry, and you miss your sister and parents. At moments, you want to give up. Yet, you worry about letting your sister and parents down. With each passing day, your dedication grows stronger.

Turn the page.

Months turn into years, and finally, you are ready. You kneel before the ceremonial altar. The piney smell and thick smoke of copal incense fills the air. The golden light of the setting sun touches your face. Your teacher marks your forehead with an obsidian blade. You are now a tlamatini.

You rise, ready to serve.

Where will your new life take you? You impressed your teachers while training and are offered a job in a temple right here in Tenochtitlan. But you were also considering looking for work as a priest in the city of Tlatelolco. It is not as busy as Tenochtitlan, and the pace of life is slower. Which will you choose?

To work in Tenochtitlan, turn to page 19.
To look for work in Tlatelolco, turn to page 35.

You decide to accept a job in a temple in Tenochtitlan. Each day, as dawn paints the sky orange and pink, you offer prayers to the gods.

Once you finish your prayers, you are ready for the day. A line of people, all looking for advice, has formed outside the temple. You help a family understand the meaning of their newborn son's birthday. You also help name him. Using the calendar system to interpret birthdates and name the children is a favorite duty among the priests.

Turn the page.

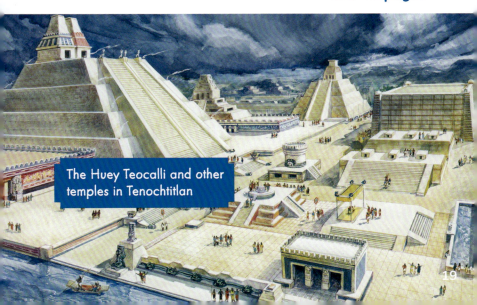

The Huey Teocalli and other temples in Tenochtitlan

When the line of people dwindles, you work at keeping the records. It is less popular work but still important. It would be a great honor to one day be invited to work on a codice, or book.

For now you are only in charge of tracking the rituals and ceremonies on a calendar. These records are used for predicting future events and passing down knowledge. They will be used to train future priests. Some of the records date back to before Tenochtitlan was built.

As the day ends, you offer one last prayer. Then, you get the feeling that someone is watching you. Glancing over your shoulder, you see a cloaked figure standing close. Their face is covered.

"Excuse me, priest." The stranger's voice is low and urgent. "I have an important message."

Out of curiosity, you rise to meet the stranger's gaze. "What is it?"

The figure leans closer. "I have an order from the new *tlatoani*. Our leader sends word that every temple must burn all the records of the old emperor," he whispers.

Your heart quickens. You've heard rumblings that the new leader wants to limit the knowledge that is available. To force people to obey without question.

Still, you can't believe he would actually order this. The records inside the temple are sacred. They contain your peoples' knowledge and history.

Before you can respond, the stranger slips away into the shadows. You feel torn between your duty to your leader and your duty to serve your people. Should you do as the stranger says or ignore him?

To burn the records, turn to page 22.
To ignore the stranger, turn to page 34.

The tlatoani is the most powerful person in the empire. You are a mere priest. You have no choice but to obey.

You grab a torch and set fire to the pages. As they curl and blacken, you are filled with guilt. These were not just records. This was the history of your people's triumphs and struggles. It was a history of their wisdom and mistakes. Now they are nothing but ash and smoke.

Without the records, your people will forget their history. They won't learn from the mistakes of the past. And if your people find out that you have set fire to these important records, they are sure to be furious.

But you are safe thanks to the new tlatoani. You were following his orders after all. He will protect you.

The crackling of the flames echoes in the quiet night. The only other sound is the occasional hiss of evaporating ink.

Then, you hear footsteps approaching behind you. You turn and see the tlatoani himself standing there. You cannot believe it! It speaks volumes that the leader would come here personally.

"You have done well, priest," the tlatoani says. "The past must give way to the present. Our future depends on it."

An ancient Aztec codex on display at the National Museum of Anthropology in Mexico City, Mexico

Turn the page.

23

You nod, seeing something in your leader's eyes that helps you understand why he ordered this. He wanted a clean slate—a new beginning.

As the last scroll turns into ash, the tlatoani turns to you with a smile. "Your dedication to me has not gone unnoticed. I have a place for you at the Huey Teocalli."

Working at the great temple is an honor like no other, but you hesitate. In addition to other priestly duties, they also perform human sacrifices there.

You know the reasoning behind the rituals—your teachers taught you about the five suns. The universe went through four different ages, each represented by a god. Each one of those gods sacrificed themselves to bring about the next age and the existence of humans.

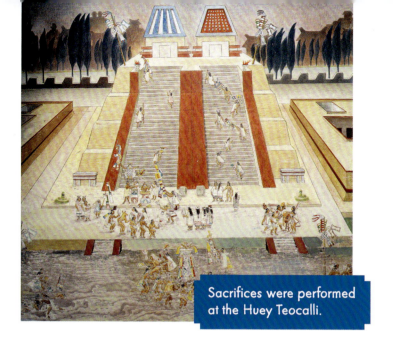

Sacrifices were performed at the Huey Teocalli.

To nourish this sun—and to thank and honor the gods for their sacrifices—the sacrifice of people is sometimes necessary. Nevertheless, you are not sure you have the stomach to work at the Huey Teocalli.

Saying yes might lead to a life full of even more difficult decisions. But saying no might be an insult. You must decide which is the lesser risk.

> To accept the tlatoani's offer, turn to page 26.
> To reject the tlatoani's offer, turn to page 29.

You decided to accept the tlatoani's offer and go work at the Huey Teocalli. A surge of emotions stirs inside you.

"I am yours to command, Tlatoani," you say, kneeling before him.

The tlatoani nods. This gesture of approval carries more weight than anything spoken. He walks away from the fading glow of the fire.

Within a month, you begin your new job at the great temple. Every morning you climb the steep, narrow steps of the temple. Climbing stairs like these is not easy, but you are determined.

At the top, you offer prayers in honor of the gods.

"Oh, great Huitzilopochtli, we turn to you to help ensure the empire prospers," you say. "Oh, gracious Tlaloc, we hope it is your will to bring rain for the crops."

Huitzilopochtli, the Aztec god of sun and war

Your duties vary. You make sure the obsidian knives are cleaned and sharpened. You also scrub the stone altars. You are new, and the more serious jobs are reserved for the high priests.

Your life is fairly predictable at first. Then, one morning, a group of captives is led onto the temple steps for sacrifice. Your breath catches in your throat. These aren't prisoners of war. They are people from Tenochtitlan.

Turn the page.

A storm of emotions threatens to give you away. "These are not prisoners of war. Why are they here?" you demand.

One of the high priests glances at you. "They were hiding some of the records that the tlatoani ordered burned. All who question his rule must be offered to the gods."

Your mind races, and your heart pounds in your chest. You've been loyal to the tlatoani. You've learned to trust that sacrifices help keep the world in balance. But now doubt claws at you. You feel torn between loyalty to your community and your duties as a high priest. Should you speak up for these people or accept that this is what the gods demand?

> To speak up, turn to page 31.
> To stay quiet, turn to page 33.

You swallow hard, unable to look at the tlatoani. You know there is a risk, but you must listen to your heart. You cannot work in the Huey Teocalli.

You kneel before your leader and speak. "I am yours to command, Tlatoani. But I cannot accept your offer."

The tlatoani's eyes narrow, and his lips set in a thin line. "Do you not see what a great honor this would be?" he says. His voice is low and dangerous. "Instead, you insult me with your rejection."

A pair of the tlatoani's men come out of the shadows. Their weapons gleam by the light of the embers.

As the men close in, you feel the cold bite of fear. You force yourself to look at the tlatoani. You wonder if he sees courage in your eyes or just stubbornness.

Turn the page.

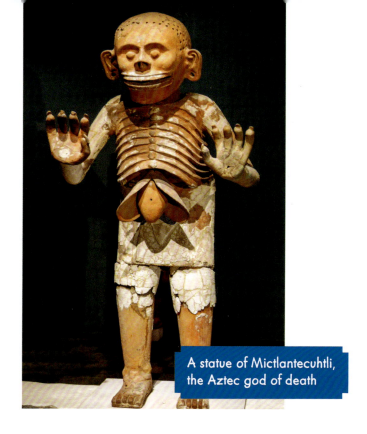

A statue of Mictlantecuhtli, the Aztec god of death

It doesn't matter either way. You will face whatever comes next with dignity. You think of your family. You think of Mictlantecuhtli, god of death. Standing by your own beliefs is the only path, even if it costs you your life.

THE END

To follow another path, turn to page 13.
To learn more about the Aztec Empire, turn to page 101.

You know you must speak up. You address the high priest once more.

"This must be a mistake," you say, your voice trembling. "You cannot sacrifice these people."

The elder looks at you. "You dare question tradition?"

You spit out the truth. "These are members of our community. I beg you to spare them."

The elder's eyes narrow. "The gods demand sacrifices to ensure our people prosper."

You know the reasoning. Still, you take a deep breath. You quietly helped the tlatoani once. Perhaps he can return the favor.

"Let me speak to the tlatoani. I've served him faithfully before," you say.

The elder priest studies you for a long moment. The weight of your words hangs in the air. Finally, he nods.

Turn the page.

"You have made a bold request," he says. "Very well. They will be spared until we can clear this up. But life in the Huey Teocalli clearly isn't for you."

As you walk away from the temple, you feel both thankful and uneasy. While you saved those people for now, a sacrifice has still been made. The high priest was right. You are not cut out for life in the Huey Teocalli. You'll have to find a new job.

THE END

To follow another path, turn to page 13.
To learn more about the Aztec Empire, turn to page 101.

You are torn between your duty as a priest and the pleas in the eyes of those prisoners. But in your culture, sacrifices are a part of life. They ensure your people prosper.

You accept that there is nothing you can do to save these people. Their lives will be given to the gods.

The prisoners are led to the altar. The high priest blows the conch horn signaling the start of the ritual. Then he speaks the sacred words. His voice is steady and commanding.

The crowd that has gathered falls silent. The obsidian knife is raised, and you close your eyes. The crowd gasps. When you open your eyes again, it is over.

You feel a deep sadness as you turn away from the temple—perhaps for good.

THE END

To follow another path, turn to page 13.
To learn more about the Aztec Empire, turn to page 101.

You know the risk you're taking, but you decide to ignore the stranger. You cannot burn the temple's records. They are too important to your people.

The fear of how the tlatoani will take your refusal is fleeting. On your walk home, a pair of men approach you. Their weapons gleam at their sides. Fear runs up your spine as you recognize the tlatoani's personal guards.

The men draw their weapons, and you brace yourself to meet the gods. In those final moments, you realize a sad truth—they will probably set fire to the records themselves. You defied the tlatoani for nothing—and it has cost you your life.

THE END

To follow another path, turn to page 13.
To learn more about the Aztec Empire, turn to page 101.

Leaving Tenochtitlan is not an easy choice. But you want a quieter life. Working at a smaller temple in Tlatelolco will give you just that.

You set off within the week and arrive in Tlatelolco just as the sun dips low in the sky. There is a warm, golden glow over the streets.

You wander around, thinking about the differences between this new city and your old one. Tlatelolco's market is larger than the one back in Tenochtitlan. Stalls filled with colorful textiles and ceramics line the streets. The vendors greet you warmly. You sense a true connection between the people who live here.

As you continue through the marketplace, the streets open up to a neighborhood. The homes here are not grand like those in Tenochtitlan. But they still have their very own gardens and courtyards.

Turn the page.

The laughter of children playing mingles with the chirping of birds. You find yourself in front of an open-air school. The lessons from the wise elder are hands-on. They teach farming techniques, crafts, and religious stories.

Farther along, you reach the small neighborhood temple. It's the reason you've come to Tlatelolco.

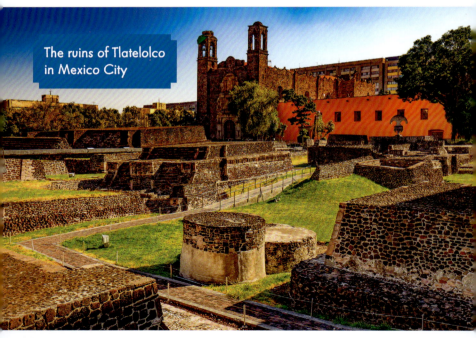

The ruins of Tlatelolco in Mexico City

You clear your throat to catch the elderly priest's attention. "Greetings, elder," you say, bowing your head slightly in respect. "I am new to the priesthood and Tlatelolco. I wish to join your temple and serve here."

After a thoughtful pause, the elder speaks. "This temple only takes on more experienced priests," he says. "Nevertheless, there are other paths to service."

You try not to show your disappointment. "I understand," you reply.

But you're unsure where to go from here. Should you take the elder priest's words to heart and look for work elsewhere in Tlatelolco? Or are you better off returning to the familiarity of Tenochtitlan?

To look for work elsewhere in Tlatelolco, turn to page 38.

To return to Tenochtitlan, turn to page 40.

You decide that you do not need to be a priest to serve your new community in Tlatelolco. You find work as a scribe instead. You dedicate yourself to recording the daily lives of your people, the seasons, and the wisdom of the elders. You make friends among the scholars, artists, and farmers.

The routine you find as the years pass is a peaceful one.

One day, an apprentice approaches you as you copy a poem. In his eyes you see the same thirst for knowledge you had in your youth.

"Master, do you ever regret leaving Tenochtitlan?" he asks. "Sometimes I ponder the choices that lie ahead of me."

You are quiet for a moment, then shake your head. "Regret can overshadow the beauty of the present. In the end, it is not the path we take that makes us, but how we walk it," you reply with a gentle smile.

Aztec scribes created written records.

The seasons continue to turn. Your once-strong hands grow frail, the lines on your face deepen, and your hair turns silver. In the company of your memories, you feel deeply grateful for the life you have lived.

THE END
To follow another path, turn to page 13.
To learn more about the Aztec Empire, turn to page 101.

Serving as a priest has always been your calling. You try every temple in Tlatelolco but hear the same answer over and over again—they are only looking for experienced priests.

Finally, you decide to return to Tenochtitlan. You are grateful to learn that there is still a place for you in the Huey Teocalli.

A stone sculpture of an Aztec priest

Each day, you thank the gods Huitzilopochtli and Tlaloc. Once you finish your prayers, you help anyone who needs it at the temple. When there are no people, you record each new birth. The birth dates will be used to help determine the outcome of each family's harvest, future prosperity, and more.

At the end of the day, you visit your sister, Yaretzi. She took a very different path from yours. She married a kindhearted farmer. They are raising a family now.

Sometimes you sit by a window together. The sounds of her children playing nearby often overtake the murmur of your conversation. You remember your own childhood together. These moments bring you the peace you once hoped to find in Tlatelolco. You do not regret returning, not for a moment.

THE END

To follow another path, turn to page 13.
To learn more about the Aztec Empire, turn to page 101.

Chapter 3
ALL THE LANDS

It's the mid-1400s in the city of Tenochtitlan, and the excited hum of your family fills the courtyard. You stand at the center of the group. You have worked hard to arrive at this moment.

Your childhood was spent helping your family in the local market. There, you learned the art of selling and trading. You eagerly watched the pochtecas—traveling merchants—arriving in the port. It was there the elders noticed your potential. They began teaching you about the world beyond Tenochtitlan.

At the age of fifteen, you became your uncle's apprentice. His job as a pochteca gave you the opportunity to learn how to check the quality of goods.

Turn the page.

You also learned what trade routes to take and the languages and customs of different places. You even accompanied your uncle on several journeys to other parts of the empire. During your last one, you handled an important trade all by yourself.

Your uncle steps forward. His eyes gleam with pride. He holds up a finely woven cloak. It is the mark of a traveling merchant, or pochteca. He places the cloak over your shoulders.

"Xilotl, you have proven your skill, your wisdom, and your dedication," he says. "Today, you finally join the ranks of the pochteca."

"Thank you, uncle," you say. "I humbly accept this role."

The crowd breaks into applause. They congratulate you and wish you well. Then, your uncle pulls you aside. He now has a serious look on his face.

"The tlatoani, our great leader, has noticed you. He has asked to meet with you," he says quietly.

"Why?" you ask. You can't believe someone so important would want to meet with you.

"He wants you to come work directly for him," your uncle responds. "You are smart, and he wants you to trade on his behalf. But between us, I suspect he also wants you to spy for him. Is this something you'd be willing to do?"

You hesitate. You've heard rumors about the life of a traveling merchant being more than just trade. Working for the great leader would be an honor, but you do not know anything about being a spy. It could be dangerous. You have a big decision to make.

To stay a merchant, turn to page 46.
To become a spy, turn to page 59.

As the first light of dawn creeps over the horizon, you meet your uncle for breakfast.

"I do not want to be a spy, uncle," you say. "Would the tlatoani consider allowing me to go on a mission to prove my worth as a merchant?"

"I will see what I can do," your uncle agrees.

Soon your uncle sends word that the tlatoani has accepted sending you on a trading journey. You will visit Cholula, a great city in the eastern lands. The tlatoani will provide goods and porters to assist you.

You set off in a week's time. It's a perfect morning, and the cool air is filled with the scent of wet earth and reeds. You pack your canoe with the finest goods the empire has to offer: shimmering jade, richly colored textiles, cacao beans, rare feathers, and delicate pottery. The porters the tlatoani provided stand ready.

Your uncle is there to see you off and shares one last piece of advice. "Remember, the tlatoani's trust is a great honor."

"Yes, uncle," you say as you step into the canoe.

You feel the familiar rock and sway of the boat beneath your feet. Your porters follow. You grasp the paddle and push off from the shore, moving with steady, practiced strokes. Tenochtitlan's grand temples and busy markets gradually fade from view.

You reach land and navigate the final leg of your journey. As you approach Cholula, towering pyramids and sprawling markets come into view once again. They rival Tenochtitlan's.

At the city's edge, a group of officials awaits. They lead you quietly through the city. The locals watch with curious eyes.

Turn the page.

You reach Cholula's square. A spread of roasted meats and fresh fruits awaits. You are seated at the place of honor, directly across from their leader, Ollin. The feast begins with performances from dancers and musicians.

"We have heard much about the wealth and power of Tenochtitlan," Ollin says.

The Great Pyramid of Cholula is the world's largest known pyramid by volume.

You gesture to the porters. "You will not be disappointed in the gifts from the tlatoani."

Ollin's eyes gleam with appreciation. "In return, we offer you precious gems and local crafts." He claps his hands, and the items are brought forth.

As the evening continues, more serious discussions begin.

"I have heard whispers of unrest to the north, in Tlaxcala," Ollin says. "Tell me—how does Tenochtitlan view these challenges?"

You consider your response carefully. You have heard the rumors as well. But you are not a diplomat. It is not your place to comment on such things.

"I am a mere merchant. But the empire has always ensured that its allies prosper and their lands are safe," you reply, choosing your words carefully.

Turn the page.

Ollin considers your response. "You don't say much, but it is wise." As you rise to leave, he adds, "You have proven yourself a worthy messenger of Tenochtitlan. I look forward to the fruits of our partnership."

"Thank you, Ollin. May our peoples thrive together in prosperity and peace," you reply, bowing deeply.

Your first mission has been a success. It is time to journey back to Tenochtitlan. Backtracking over land and water is the longer but sure way home. There is also a shorter route completely by land. You'll have to cut across the mountains on narrow trails. Some call it dangerous, but it will allow you to share the news of your success with the tlatoani much quicker. Which route will you choose?

To take the shortcut home, turn to page 51.

To take the long but sure way home, turn to page 57.

You cannot wait to share the news of your success and decide to take the shortcut home. Your porters help you navigate through narrow trails that wind dangerously close to steep cliffs.

As you make your way along one narrow ledge, the ground beneath you suddenly shifts. Loose rocks give way. You and one of your porters lose your footing.

Before you can catch yourself, you tumble down the slope. The world spins around you in a blur of green and gray. You desperately try to grasp onto something to break your fall, but there is nothing.

Finally, you hit the ground. Pain radiates through your body. You lie there, breathless and bruised. By some miracle, you are alive. Your porter, on the other hand, has died from the fall.

Turn the page.

As you struggle to get up, shadowy figures emerge from behind the trees. They quickly overwhelm your group.

Your first instinct is to fight back. But something tells you that you might have a better chance of survival if you let them take the gifts Ollin gave you for the tlatoani. You must make your next move quickly.

To fight back, turn to page 53.
To offer up the tlatoani's gifts, turn to page 55.

You try to fight back, but one of the attackers strikes you down with a sharp, heavy rock. Darkness takes over.

When you wake, your attackers are gone—and so are Ollin's gifts. They were stolen from you. Your efforts to save them were pointless.

Pain shoots through your body as you try to stand. You decide you cannot return to Tenochtitlan empty-handed. You will be punished or shamed. Instead, you travel deeper into the mountains.

Turn the page.

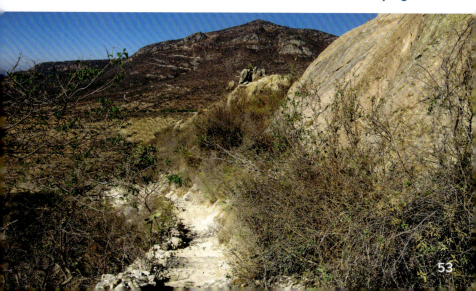

The journey is slow and difficult. Every step is a reminder of the treacherous shortcut and the attack.

Finally, you stumble onto a small village. You feel relief—until you recognize your baskets discarded outside a nearby dwelling.

You realize you have stumbled straight into danger. These are the same people who attacked you on the trail. You are as good as dead.

THE END

To follow another path, turn to page 13.
To learn more about the Aztec Empire, turn to page 101.

You stand before your attackers, heart racing.

"Please. If you kill us, you undermine the peace we strive for," you plead. "Take these goods as a sign of goodwill. They symbolize our alliance and respect."

One of the attackers, a tall man, steps forward, eyes narrowed. "You've intruded on our territory."

"We meant no harm," you insist.

You signal for the porters to bring out the gifts Ollin sent for the tlatoani. Your attackers examine them carefully.

"You're bold for a pochteca," the tall man finally says. "Very well, we'll accept and offer our alliance in turn."

You and your porters leave the encounter empty-handed but relieved. You will get to see your families again.

Turn the page.

Word of your return to Tenochtitlan spreads quickly. Soon you are called to see the tlatoani for the first time. He listens to your tale with a serious face, then places a hand on your shoulder. It is a gesture of respect and reassurance.

"The physical riches may be lost, pochteca. However, the value of your journey lies in the alliances you have brought back. This experience has proven your worth," he says.

You nod in understanding. The riches may be gone, but your new favor with the tlatoani is far greater.

THE END

To follow another path, turn to page 13.
To learn more about the Aztec Empire, turn to page 101.

As tempting as it is to take the short way home, you're not willing to risk your life—or those of your men. Packed with treasures, you begin the journey back to Tenochtitlan. Many nights are spent under starry skies.

Finally, Tenochtitlan's grand temples come back into view. Upon your return, the tlatoani waits for you. You meet with him in his chambers.

"It is a great honor to meet you," you say, bowing deeply. You begin to recount the journey, humbly bragging about the successful trade agreements and a potential alliance with Ollin.

As you speak, the tlatoani's face shifts from curious to satisfied. He places one hand on your shoulder and gestures to one of his men with the other. The man steps forward carrying a heavy bag.

Turn the page.

"Rise, pochteca," the tlatoani says to you. "Take these riches as a thanks. Continue to serve our empire with the same dedication, and your future will be bright."

You feel the weight of the reward. "Thank you, great tlatoani."

As you leave the palace, you smile. You're not just happy that you have gained favor with the leader. You also know that your new riches will make your future much more comfortable.

THE END

To follow another path, turn to page 13.
To learn more about the Aztec Empire, turn to page 101.

Spying is dangerous work, but this is an opportunity to serve the tlatoani and your people. You ask your uncle to arrange a meeting with the leader. Soon he sends word—you have been summoned to the tlatoani's chambers.

When you arrive, the tlatoani is waiting for you. "Pochteca, we have heard whispers of unrest and secret alliances to the east, in Tlaxcala," he says. "We need eyes and ears to confirm these rumors."

You take a deep breath. This calms the nerves fluttering in your chest. You bow deeply. "I am honored by your trust, great tlatoani. I will gather the information you seek."

The tlatoani nods. "Remember, no one must know why you are really there. Blend in and trade as usual, but keep your senses sharp. Return when you have something to report. The safety and prosperity of our empire depend on it."

Turn the page.

You prepare for the journey carefully. Alongside the usual trade items—jade carvings, colorful textiles, and cacao beans—you hide a set of papers and inks. These will be used to record what you see and hear. You also choose your porters carefully. You need to make sure that they'll keep quiet about your true mission.

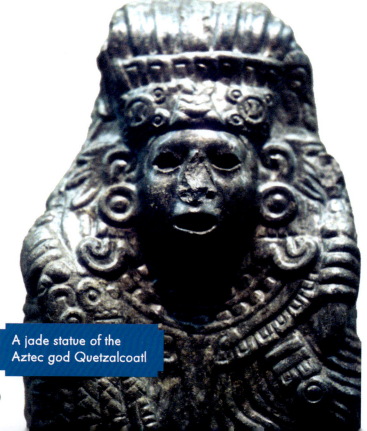

A jade statue of the Aztec god Quetzalcoatl

You travel through jungles and mountains. Along the way, you keep up with your duties as a pochteca. You trade but always with an eye and ear for information. In each village, you talk to people normally. As you do, you listen for hints of unrest or secret dealings.

Your journey takes you to the city of Cholula. You head straight for the busy market. You present the local merchants with the goods you've brought—items chosen to showcase the wealth and craftsmanship of Tenochtitlan.

In return, the merchants offer you precious beads and beautiful woven textiles. You gladly accept them, but it is the innocent conversations that have real value. The talk between a group of men at a nearby fish stand catches your attention. Their hushed tones and eye-shifting suggest they are discussing something they don't want others to know.

Turn the page.

You shift closer, pretending to examine the fresh catch as you strain to listen to their conversation.

"I'm telling you, we can't keep living under Tenochtitlan's thumb," the first man whispers, glancing around nervously.

A second man, his voice low and urgent, replies, "I've heard there are groups in the north ready to rise against them. If we join forces, we could finally stand a chance."

A third man, older and more cautious, interjects, "With greater numbers, we could present a real threat."

The first man sighs, rubbing his chin thoughtfully. "And how do you propose we make contact with these groups?"

The second man leans in closer. "I know someone who's been in touch with them. We can arrange a meeting, but we need to be smart about it."

"Agreed," the third man says, his voice steady.

As their voices fade, you step back. This is the proof the tlatoani needs—an alliance is forming against Tenochtitlan.

Your heart races as you ask one of your men—a scribe sent to help keep records—to write down these details later that night. The rumors the tlatoani warned you about are true!

You must return home immediately. But it is nighttime. Leaving under the cover of darkness might help you go unnoticed, but it might also raise suspicions. What will you do?

To leave under the cover of night, turn to page 64.
To wait and leave by daylight, turn to page 70.

You decide to travel at night so you can get home as soon as possible. You will backtrack by land and then water. Gathering your men, you hide the treasures and precious spy scrolls. They are the fruits of your dangerous mission.

The dense forest is very quiet. The only sounds are the rustle of leaves and the distant calls of nocturnal animals. Your small group moves carefully.

Suddenly, other men—silent and swift—come out of the darkness. Before you can react, you and your porters are surrounded. The attackers' faces are fierce. The moonlight glints off their weapons. A brief struggle takes place, but you are outnumbered and outmatched.

Your attackers bind your hands tightly and rummage through your belongings. Their rough hands tear through the carefully packed goods.

When they find the papers with your notes, their leader's eyes narrow with suspicion and anger. He quickly scans its contents, and something changes in his face.

"Are you a spy?" he demands.

You have a choice. You can lie and hope the men believe you. Or you can tell the truth and try to talk your way out of this situation. What will you do?

To take your chances with a lie, turn to page 66.
To tell the truth, turn to page 68.

"I am a simple merchant," you lie.

But there is no convincing your captors. They have seen the papers where you wrote your observations for the tlatoani.

"I was not born yesterday. A simple merchant would not risk the danger of travel by night," their leader says.

They drag you and your porters to a nearby village. It is small compared to Cholula and Tenochtitlan but well-protected. You are all thrown into a dark, damp hole in the ground.

As the cold darkness surrounds you, the reality of your capture sinks in. The papers, the key to your mission, are now in the hands of your captors.

Days blur together as you sit in the hole. Your captors occasionally give you food. When they interrogate you, you are are silent. You don't have much to say that isn't already on the pages they took.

The fear of what might come next gnaws at you. Will you be put to death as a spy?

Your captors grow frustrated with your lack of information. The time since your last meal grows longer and longer. The ants become your dinner. You realize they don't have to kill you—you have all been left in that hole to die.

THE END

To follow another path, turn to page 13.
To learn more about the Aztec Empire, turn to page 101.

"Yes, I am a spy," you confess, hoping to talk your way out of it. "But I mean no harm to Cholula or to you. I only meant to learn more about what was happening south of here."

"It does not look good on us to let you cross through our lands to spy on our neighbors," the leader says.

You think quickly. "I will pay you for your troubles," you tell him. "Take the goods I carry with me. They are an act of goodwill from the tlatoani himself."

The leader hesitates, then nods.

"We don't want any part of whatever is brewing. Leave the goods, and don't ever come back," he says.

You and your porters hurry home, grateful to be alive. You hope the goods do not matter—your true mission was to gather information.

Upon your return, you are summoned by the tlatoani. You kneel before him and recount the attack on your men.

"Was I wrong to give them the goods in exchange for my men's lives, great leader?" you ask.

The tlatoani places his hand on your shoulder. "Rise, pochteca. Your true mission wasn't the trade. It was the knowledge you gathered. You made a smart move. Your future with the empire is bright."

"Thank you, great tlatoani," you say. You walk home, looking forward to this future.

THE END

To follow another path, turn to page 13.
To learn more about the Aztec Empire, turn to page 101.

You want to go home immediately, but leaving in the middle of the night would be too suspicious. You decide to wait until the next day.

At first light you set off, backtracking by land and then water. As Tenochtitlan's grand temples finally come back into view, you feel triumphant. You've made it.

As soon as you arrive, you are called to the tlatoani's chambers. You bow deeply, presenting the treasures from Cholula. Then, you hand him the papers containing your observations.

"The rumors are true, great tlatoani. There is unrest in the east. A coalition is forming against our empire," you say. Your voice is steady but urgent.

The tlatoani studies the pages. "Our empire owes you a great debt, pochteca."

An Aztec tlatoani was both a priest and ruler.

He rewards you with a position as his official spy. You aren't able to tell your uncle you will no longer be able to work beside him. Yet, you are excited for your next mission.

THE END

To follow another path, turn to page 13.
To learn more about the Aztec Empire, turn to page 101.

Chapter 4
GROWING DISCONTENT

It is the early 1500s, and the empire's leader, the tlatoani, has called on a handful of trusted people to help with his conquered territories. Your father, a calpixque, is chosen to go to the coastal city of Cempoala.

You and your family leave Tenochtitlan with all your belongings. The landscape changes dramatically as you move east. The air grows warmer. The vegetation grows denser. Palm trees sway, and the ocean sings.

The place is warm, but the glances of the locals are cold. They look at you and your family with suspicion. They have been under Aztec rule for some fifty years, and you are the face of the empire.

Turn the page.

Your mother quickly gets to work, setting up your new home. Meanwhile, your father begins his new duties. Most days, you help him. You walk through the busy streets of Cempoala carrying a scroll to make sure that all tributes are accounted for.

You don't just learn the importance of record-keeping. You learn the tribute system and the types of goods and services required from the people. You also help deal with the locals.

"Our duty is not just to collect," your father tells you. "We must also understand and balance the needs of the people with those of Tenochtitlan."

As the seasons change, and the years pass, the people of Cempoala start to see you not just as your father's assistant, but as a capable tribute collector in your own right. Then your father's health takes a downward turn.

One evening, he calls to you from his deathbed.

"The time has come," he says, his voice weak. "You must take over as calpixque. Be fair and just."

With that, he is gone. Your mourning time is brief, as you must get right to work. As the eldest child, your father's job now falls to you.

You have never collected the tributes by yourself before. You are not sure if people will welcome you. You must choose your first collection carefully. The farmers have always treated you kindly. The merchants can sometimes be difficult. Who will you visit first?

To collect tribute from a farmer, turn to page 76.
To collect tribute from a merchant, turn to page 78.

You decide to visit a local farmer named Kuxi. While collecting the monthly tribute of maize and cacao beans, you notice his eyes look tired. Sensing he is upset, you pause.

"Kuxi, you seem troubled," you say. "Is there something you wish to discuss?"

He hesitates before speaking. "My family struggles to meet the demands of the empire. The tribute takes a heavy toll on our harvest. Many in the village feel the same." He pauses. "We told your father this before he died. Maybe now that you are in charge you can help."

You are quiet. Your father never spoke to you about this. But maybe this is why he brought up fairness and justice on his deathbed.

Finally, you speak. "I thank you for confiding in me, Kuxi. I will see what others have to say about this." With that, you excuse yourself.

You walk home, deep in thought. You know there is a balance you must maintain. Tenochtitlan depends on the tributes you collect, but the well-being of the people in Cempoala is equally important.

You wish more than ever that your father was here to advise you. But this is a choice you must make on your own. You make a list of who else to speak to and set off to get answers.

Turn to page 80.

You decide to visit a local merchant named Aktzin. When you knock on a door, a middle-aged man opens it. Worry lines his face.

"Good day," you say, greeting the merchant with respect. "I am here to collect this month's tribute. You owe two sacks of maize and a bundle of cotton textiles."

Aktzin sighs deeply. He knows why you have come. "Please, come in. I will gather the goods."

As you wait, you overhear Aktzin's wife in the next room. "Your sister's children go hungry while we give more and more to our conquerors. Something must change. Maybe having a new calpixque is an opportunity to be heard," she whispers.

Aktzin's voice is low but firm. "I will not make those types of demands on this child. Disobedience will only bring the anger of the tlatoani upon us."

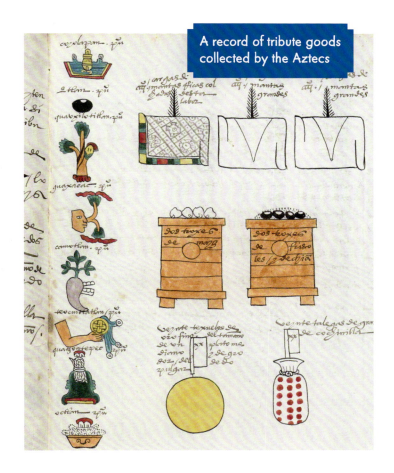

A record of tribute goods collected by the Aztecs

You frown at what you've overheard. Aktzin means well in trying to protect you, but you are not a child. You silently vow to investigate this matter further to prove it. You need to talk to some of the other neighbors.

Turn to page 80.

79

Over the coming days, you meet with others. You see and hear the same frustrations.

An elderly woman, bent with age, hands you a small bundle of cacao beans. Her life's work is contained in that small offering.

A young man, barely out of his teens, parts with a portion of his harvest. You accept it but see the unspoken anger in his eyes.

One morning, you stumble onto a group that has gathered in the central square. There is tension in the air. A man steps forward. It is Manixná, one of the first friends you made when you arrrived in Cempoala. His face has grown hard.

"Something must change," Manixná says loudly, his voice carrying through the square. "We work endlessly, yet we see little benefit. The empire takes and takes, leaving us with barely enough to survive."

You step forward as well, meeting his gaze. "The tributes are necessary. Without them, the empire cannot protect and provide for all of you." You speak calmly, trying to remain in control of the situation.

A murmur ripples through the crowd. Manixná steps closer, his eyes flashing with anger.

"But at what cost?" he demands. "The larger part of our harvest is sent off to Tenochtitlan. How long do you expect us to put up with this?"

As a calpixque, you are the face of the empire in Cempoala. But you also feel for your neighbors. You have a difficult choice to make: talk to your superiors in Tenochtitlan or continue to collect the tributes as usual.

To speak to your superiors in Tenochtitlan, turn to page 82.
To collect tributes as usual, turn to page 85.

The voices of Cempoala are growing louder and more urgent.

"I will report your concerns to my superiors. Maybe they'll make some changes," you say, trying to offer hope.

Manixná studies you for a long moment. Finally, he nods slowly. "We will hold you to that."

As the day ends, you begin your journey to Tenochtitlan. You are determined to keep your word and speak with your superiors.

Soon, you see the familiar landscape of your former home. Tenochtitlan never fails to awe you. The busy markets, towering temples, and shimmering canals are impressive. But today, there is no time to admire the scenery. You head straight to the temples to speak with the tlatoani.

"Honorable leader," you begin, "I have come to discuss the situation in Cempoala.

The people are struggling. They cannot keep up with the tributes."

The tlatoani looks irritated, but you stand your ground.

"If we do not address this, we risk rebellion," you warn.

"Rebellion? You underestimate the power of our empire. The tributes are needed to maintain prosperity and military strength. Your duty is to collect, not to question. Return to Cempoala and remind the people of their duty." He dismisses you with a wave.

You bow your head, realizing that your request has fallen on deaf ears. As you leave Tenochtitlan, a heavy sense of disappointment falls over you.

You return to Cempoala and tell your neighbors what the tlatoani said. You are only the messenger, but your neighbors see this as a broken promise.

Turn the page.

Manixná drags you toward an empty structure that has been repurposed as a prison and throws you inside. Your life as a calpixque is over. You will spend the rest of your days in this jail.

THE END

To follow another path, turn to page 13.
To learn more about the Aztec Empire, turn to page 101.

Despite the growing unrest, you know you have a duty to the empire. You continue to collect the tributes.

One afternoon, as you make your rounds, you notice an angry crowd outside the school. You try to retreat, but they close in around you.

Manixná steps forward. "We cannot continue like this," he says. "No more."

Before you can respond, strong hands grab you from behind. The people have planned this moment well. Panic surges through you as you are dragged toward an empty structure that has been repurposed as a prison.

You are thrown onto the cold dirt floor of a cell. There is nothing to do but listen as the sound of footsteps fades, leaving you in silence.

Days pass slowly. From your cell, you overhear bits of conversations. You recognize the voices of some of your neighbors who have been tasked with guarding you.

Turn the page.

"If we hit them hard and fast, we might catch them off guard," one of them says, his tone tinged with excitement.

"We need to have a better strategy than throwing ourselves at their walls," says a second person.

"Strategy?" the first one scoffs. "What's the point of all this if we don't act? Sitting here and waiting is a death sentence for us too!"

One evening, Manixná approaches you. He looks at you with a mixture of anger and pity.

"You could have listened. You could have helped us. This is what you get for ignoring us," he says quietly.

You nod, understanding the truth in his words. "I see that now," you admit. "I was wrong to dismiss you."

Manixná studies you for a moment before turning away. "You were always a smart one. Perhaps you'll still think of a way out of this."

As you sit alone in the dark, you consider his words. Is he right? Is there still a way out? You wonder if escape to Tenochtitlan is possible. Or, maybe you can save yourself by finding a way to help the people of Cempoala.

To flee to Tenochtitlan, turn to page 88.
To find a way to help Cempoala, turn to page 91.

You know your only chance for survival is to escape to Tenochtitlan. Fear gives way to a plan. You recognize one of the guards. He is an old friend of your father's.

"Please help me," you beg.

The guard appears to ignore you. But that evening, he returns and unlocks the door to your prison.

"Run west," he whispers. "The terrain is rough, but it's your best hope."

"Thank you," you whisper back as you sneak through the shadows.

The familiar streets are a maze of danger. When you reach the edge of Cempoala, you take one last look at the place that has been your home. Your mother is still there. You whisper a silent prayer for her safety, promising to find a way to come back for her someday.

Travel to the west by land is unforgiving. Dense forests give way to rocky hills, and you have to navigate these treacherous paths in the dark. Every step is a struggle, but the thought of freedom keeps you moving.

Without supplies, you drink from streams and forage for food. Exhaustion and hunger gnaw at you but you push onward. The nights are cold, and the days are a blur of walking. Somehow you avoid being followed.

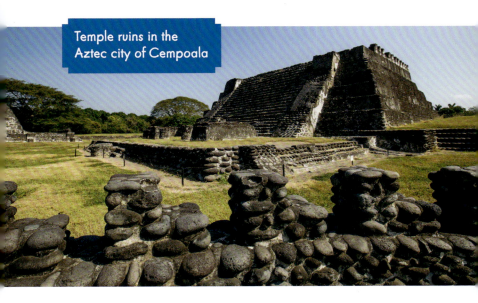

Temple ruins in the Aztec city of Cempoala

Turn the page.

As you trudge forward, your mind wanders back to your family. You think of your father's wisdom and your mother's gentle touch. She must now fend for herself on her own.

Finally, after what feels like an eternity, you reach Tenochtitlan. You report what happened. The tlatoani is angry.

"I see now that we should not have let a boy do a man's job," he says.

He assigns someone to replace you. Now that you have been removed from service, your mother is forced to give up her home in Cempoala and return to Tenochtitlan. This is upsetting, but at least you are all safe.

THE END

To follow another path, turn to page 13.
To learn more about the Aztec Empire, turn to page 101.

The desire to escape is strong, but the risk is great. And the thought of leaving your mother behind is unbearable. You must stay and try to help the people of Cempoala.

The next morning, as the sun rises, you ask to speak with Manixná.

"What is it you want?" he asks, looking annoyed.

"I understand your anger. I want to help. I want to fight with you," you declare.

Manixná studies you for a long moment, weighing your words. Something convinces him to let you out. Maybe it is the memory of your friendship. Still, he offers a warning. "If you betray us, there will be no mercy."

You walk to the square, a free man, and stand among the people of Cempoala. You publicly reject your role as a calpixque, pledging to stand with your neighbors against the might of Tenochtitlan.

Turn the page.

That evening, you return to your family's home. Your mother hugs you tightly.

"Are you sure about this? What will happen when the tlatoani finds out?" she asks, her voice trembling.

You take a deep breath. "They will be angry, but I have made up my mind. Cempoala has been more of a home to me than Tenochtitlan ever was. I want to help rebuild our lives here."

In the months that follow, you trade your official robes for simple farming clothes. You till the land, plant crops, and tend the fields.

The Aztecs farmed corn, also called maize.

The work is hard but fulfilling. The people of Cempoala slowly begin to accept you as one of their own.

Despite the peace you find in your new life, you know that the empire will not let this uprising go unpunished. They will send another calpixque, and with him, reinforcements to crush the rebellion.

You know the time is coming near. Tenochtitlan will come, and they will outnumber you. You must advise Manixná. Will you tell him to seek out a new alliance, or wait and let the gods decide?

>To suggest a new alliance, turn to page 94.
>To wait it out, turn to page 97.

That evening, you spot strange vessels off the coast and take it as a sign. Cempoala is ready for a new alliance.

You talk to Manixná, and he is in agreement. He gathers your neighbors in the central square.

"I know you are all wondering about these vessels," Manixná begins. "Where you see strangers, I see possibilities. These strangers can be our allies."

You step forward. "For our families—and our future," you declare.

You offer the newcomers friendship. They are from a place on the other side of the coast—a land they call España. They speak a language they call Spanish and ride animals they call horses.

The newcomers have a plan to attack Tenochtitlan. It is as if the gods have sent these strangers. You agree to fight beside them.

After a few weeks, you find yourself marching with them toward Tenochtitlan. The Tlaxcalans and other cities conquered by the Aztec Empire stand beside you.

The clash with Tenochtitlan's army is brutal. The Spanish have metal armor and powerful weapons they call cannons. The air is filled with the cries of warriors and the thunder of these weapons.

You fight hard, but the cost is high. You see Manixná fall, struck down by a spear. Your friend lies wounded, clutching his side. You watch in horror as he takes his last breath, but there is no time to grieve. The screams of your neighbors and the desperate shouts of the Spanish commanders overwhelm you.

After the battle, you join the Spanish on the retreat from Tenochtitlan. The night is dark. The only light comes from the torches that flicker in the hands of your companions.

Turn the page.

The retreat quickly turns into chaos. As you cross one of the raised roads leading out of the city, warriors from the empire launch another fierce attack. Arrows rain down, and warriors surge from the shadows.

You are struck by an arrow and fall into the lake, your cry echoing in the night. You struggle to reach the surface, but the water is too deep. You are weakened and devastated. You have lost your neighbors, your friend, everything. The empire will surely punish everyone in Cempoala for this attack.

You have nothing left to fight for. It's the last thought you have before you let the lake swallow you.

THE END

To follow another path, turn to page 13.
To learn more about the Aztec Empire, turn to page 101.

You are at peace with what you have in your life, so you decide to wait and see what Tenochtitlan does next. Perhaps the gods will send you a sign. Then something unexpected happens.

Massive vessels anchor just off the coast. This sends waves of unease throughout Cempoala. Are these newcomers your potential salvation or just another tyrant?

You and your neighbors gather to decide what to do next.

"They could be our chance to break free from Tenochtitlan," one man says.

Manixná stands tall and says what you've been thinking: "We must be cautious. These strangers could bring more harm than good."

You step forward and take a deep breath, choosing your words carefully. "Manixná is right. We must watch them first, learn their ways, and understand their intentions."

Turn the page.

A woman crosses her arms and glares at you. "And how long will that take?"

"We will send a delegation to meet with them before the next moon," Manixná replies.

The crowd slowly makes their way home. Some are still grumbling, but many are nodding in agreement. You can't help feeling a knot in your stomach. The newcomers could change everything—for better or worse.

The next day, you and a few chosen men approach the newcomers' camp. The sight of their metal armor and strange weapons makes you nervous, but you offer food and drink as a gesture of goodwill. You find out they call themselves Spaniards.

Their leader speaks through an interpreter. His words are smooth, and his mannerisms are confident.

"We come in peace and seek allies," he says.

You trade glances with Manixná. The words are promising, but the truth remains to be seen. As you return to Cempoala, you feel the weight of the decision pressing down.

Then, the newcomers' sickness comes—a disease they call smallpox. It spreads like wildfire through Cempoala.

You fall ill. Fever wracks your body, leaving you delirious and weak. When you finally get better, you see that many of your neighbors have not survived. You look at your reflection in the water. Your face and body are covered in scars. The marks of the disease are proof that the Spaniards cannot be trusted.

You wish you had all continued paying tributes to the empire for their protection. You have a feeling that you're going to need it.

THE END

To follow another path, turn to page 13.
To learn more about the Aztec Empire, turn to page 101.

Chapter 5
THE LEGACY OF A FALLEN EMPIRE

The Aztec Empire began its rise in the early 1300s. For the next 200 years, the Aztecs—or Mexica, as they called themselves—conquered neighboring people. They also formed alliances with neighboring peoples throughout central Mexico. This helped the empire become large and powerful.

The conquered peoples paid tributes—similar to taxes—with goods or work. This funded the growth of Tenochtitlan—the capital city. It served as the center of trade, politics, and religion. The tribues also allowed the Aztecs to build impressive structures like the Huey Teocalli, a massive pyramid dedicated to two of the most important Aztec gods.

The capital's further expansion was made possible by the use of chinampas. This technique of turning marshy land into floating farms allowed the Aztecs to increase usable land and support a population of more than 200,000 people.

Chinampas allowed the Aztecs to create more farming space.

The Aztecs felt they owed their success to their gods. To repay the gods, they made sacrifices. The common practice was to offer gifts, such as flowers, pottery, and art. But sometimes humans were sacrificed. The Aztecs believed these sacrifices and offerings helped balance the world. This was part of their religion.

The arrival of the Spanish in 1519 signaled the beginning of the end. The Aztecs welcomed the Spanish, hoping it would lessen the threat. But soon conflict erupted. Conquered people—like those in Cempoala— had grown resentful toward the Aztecs. They allied with the Spanish.

In 1520, the Aztecs pushed the Spanish out of Tenochtitlan. But the victory didn't last. The Spanish had brought smallpox with them. The disease killed both enemies and allies.

Across the empire, faith in the tlatoani lessened. The Spanish were able to recruit more allies to attack the now weakened Tenochtitlan again. After many battles, the city fell on August 13, 1521.

After conquering many people, the Aztecs were now the conquered. After the fall of the Aztec Empire, the Spanish built Mexico City, Mexico, on the ruins of Tenochtitlan. They forced their own culture and government on the Aztecs. This brought many changes, including Christianity, new farming techniques, and new forms of art and architecture. Holidays like Día de los Muertos—Day of the Dead—arose from a blend of Christianity and Aztec religion.

Aztec history is ever present in Mexico City's markets, landmarks, and museums. Moreover, an estimated 1.5 million people in central Mexico still speak Nahuatl, the language of the Aztecs. Words with roots

Performers celebrate at a Day of the Dead parade in Mexico City.

in Nahuatl—including chocolate, tomato, avocado, and chili—are used every day.

Just as Aztec culture helped shape Mexico's identity, it also helped shape the identity of Mexican Americans. It ties Mexican Americans to the United States through Aztlan—the original Aztec homeland in the Southwest. Native culture didn't disappear. It just adapted.

TIMELINE OF THE AZTEC EMPIRE

1100—The Aztec people leave their homeland of Aztlan.

1200—The Aztecs arrive in the Valley of Mexico.

1325—The Aztecs settle in Lake Texcoco and establish Tenochtitlan.

1376—Acamapichtli, the first major ruler of the Aztecs, comes into power. He is given the title tlatoani or "speaker."

1428—Under the rule of Itzcoatl, the Aztecs begin forming alliances with nearby cities in Texcoco and Tlacopan.

1440—Montezuma I begins his reign. He extends the boundaries of the Aztec Empire to the Gulf of Mexico.

1452—Tenochtitlan faces flooding, drought, and famine. These disasters set off the Flower Wars, ceremonial battles that provided captives for the Aztecs and their enemies to sacrifice.

1487—The Huey Teocalli is expanded and dedicated in honor of Ahuitzotl's reign.

1502—Moctezuma II begins his reign. The Aztec Empire grows to its largest extent. Some people living within the empire begin to resent the growing demands for tributes.

1519—Spanish explorer Hernán Cortés arrives in Mexico and begins forming alliances with cities unhappy with Aztec rule.

1520—The Spanish and their allies attack Tenochtitlan but are forced to retreat. A smallpox outbreak strikes the Aztecs.

1521—Cortés and his allies succeed in capturing Tenochtitlan.

1522—The Spanish begin building a new city on the ruins of Tenochtitlan. They intend to call it Mexico City and make it the capital of New Spain.

MORE ABOUT THE AZTEC EMPIRE

>>> The Aztecs believed in many gods, but the most important were Huitzilopochtli—the god of war and fire—and Tlaloc—the god of rain. The Huey Teocalli, or great temple, was a massive pyramid dedicated to these two gods. It is referred to as the "Templo Mayor" in Spanish. Its ruins can be found in the heart of modern-day Mexico City.

>>> The Aztecs used two main calendars. One was the tonalpohualli, a 260-day ritual calendar. The other was the xiuhpohualli, a 365-day calendar that accurately measured the same solar year that we use with our modern calendar. Once every 52 years, the start of the new year lined up on these calendars. Some believed this could signal the end of the world.

>>> The Aztecs grew and ate maize, beans, chilies, tomatoes, squash, cacao, and cacti as part of their regular diet. People still eat and cook with these foods today.

>>> The markets in Tenochtitlan were an important part of life. They drew as many as 50,000 people in a day.

>>> By the time the Spaniards arrived in 1519, the Aztec Empire was home to some six million people. Between one-quarter and one-half of those living in the Aztec Empire died of smallpox brought to the region by Europeans.

THE AZTEC EMPIRE TODAY

Today, Tenochtitlan is buried under modern-day Mexico City. Some 21 million residents walk just above the ruins of this ancient Aztec city every day. Subway riders who pass through the Pino Suarez metro station, for example, walk directly past a small Aztec temple built to honor to the wind god, Ehecatl.

The ruins of the Huey Teocalli in Mexico City

Archaeologists are eager to study the ruins of Tenochtitlan. But excavation—the process of uncovering a buried city—has not been easy for a city built atop a lake. The city is sinking, and the landscape is prone to earthquakes. The ruins of the Huey Teocalli remained buried until extensive excavation began in 1978.

Today, new discoveries are made regularly, including:

2015—Renovation of a building behind a cathedral in Mexico City leads archaeologists to uncover a giant skull rack where the Mexica displayed the skulls of their sacrificial victims. Nearly 700 skulls are also uncovered.

2017—Renovation of a Mexico City hotel uncovers an ancient ōllamalīztli court. Ball games played on theses courts had religious meaning.

2022—Archaeologists still digging at the Huey Teocalli discover the bones of a sacrificed jaguar.

Chalchiuhtlicue, the Aztec water goddess

The search for more artifacts has evolved with the use of technology, including lidar—Light Detection and Ranging. This scanning technology is used to locate artifacts in their original locations. Many of the artifacts found at these archaeological sites are now showcased in museums.

GLOSSARY

alliance (uh-LY-uhnts)—an agreement between groups to work together

apprentice (uh-PREN-tiss)—someone who learns a trade by working with a skilled person

chinampa (chi-NAM-puh)—a floating meadow or garden created on a lake or pond by piling soil pulled from the bottom onto a mat of twigs

coalition (koh-uh-LISH-uhn)—an alliance of people, groups, or countries working together toward a common goal

conquer (KAHNG-kuhr)—to defeat and take control by force

delegation (de-li-GAY-shuhn)—a group chosen to represent others

empire (EM-pire)—a large territory ruled by a powerful leader

obsidian (uhb-SID-ee-uhn)—a dark, glasslike rock formed by cooling volcanic lava

porter (POR-tur)—a person hired to carry heavy loads or goods

prosper (PROS-per)—to become strong and flourishing

rebellion (ri-BEL-yuhn)—a fight against those in power

scribe (SKRIBE)—a person who copies books, letters, contracts, and other documents by hand

terrain (tuh-RAYN)—the surface of the land

textile (TEK-stile)—a woven or knit cloth

tyrant (TYE-ruhnt)—someone who rules other people in a cruel or unjust way

READ MORE

Williams, Brian. *Maya, Incas, and Aztecs.* New York: DK Publishing, 2018.

Yasuda, Anita. *Ancient Civilizations: Aztecs, Maya, Incas!* White River Junction, VT: Nomad Press, 2019.

INTERNET SITES

Britannica Kids: Aztec
kids.britannica.com/kids/article/Aztec/352810

Ducksters: Aztec Empire: Daily Life
ducksters.com/history/aztec_empire/daily_life.php

National Geographic Kids: Aztec Civilization
kids.nationalgeographic.com/history/article/aztec-civilization

ABOUT THE AUTHOR

Claudia Oviedo is a Mexican American author who heard a lot about Aztec history growing up. She writes for children under various names and enjoys books that make history fun. Honors include: 2009 Paterson Prize for Books for Young People, as well as the 2008 and 2015 Texas Institute of Letters Best Young Adult Book Award, and several starred reviews.

BOOKS IN THIS SERIES

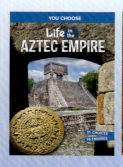
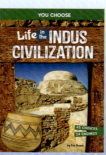
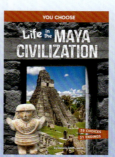